THE REAL INCONVENIENT TRUTH

Predictions of a dead man

To the memory of my father

John Layton Green, Jr.

www.jgreenbooks.com

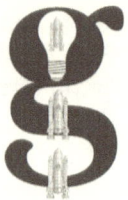

INTRODUCTION

Pollution, global warming, disease, war, famine, corruption, genetic defects, decaying urban areas, and religious zealotry - These are only a few problems facing humanity today and they all have the same root cause. Most predicted and the cause identified over a half century ago by a man long dead. Long before computers, the internet, social media and the technological explosion of the 21st century he cataloged, graphed, spoke and wrote about it. This author listened attentively and studied the graphs and notes he kept in three-ring binders because I knew the man well.

Mostly, however, I remembered his observations about the future of human kind. Probably very similar to countless barstool philosophers except he never said, "what they ought to do is..." or "the only solution to it is..." In his way of thinking, there *was* no solution. The world was pretty much done for and it was just a matter of time until we all realized it, but most wouldn't realize it even then, because they were too ignorant and selfish. "It will happen," he said, "you can count on it."

Moreover, he continually reinforced what he considered to be, the root cause, the problem that created or amplified all other problems facing the world. Had he access to the internet or social media, he would have more information but no real surprises. This author however, has such access and much data accumulated is included in this book. Read it if you dare and draw your own conclusions.

GEOMETRIC PROGRESSION "Johnny... what would you take? A million dollars right now or a penny doubled every day for a month?" I knew the answer by rote. Depending on the month, this would work out to a difference between 1.3 million or 10 million bucks. I had heard this question and the variables on geometric progression from my dad almost as many times I had heard his old army stories.

"Everything in history is moving at an ever increasing pace. For five THOUSAND years, people rode around on horses, donkeys and camels. Then, 150 years or so ago came steamboats, trolley cars and trains. Then less than a hundred years ago came the first automobile. You had to hand-crank them to start them and drain the water out of them every day when it was below freezing outside. Twenty-five miles an hour was breakneck speed back then. Now you can barely get on the road without some idiot blasting by you at 60, 80 or 100 miles an hour. Airplanes too. The Wright Brother flew 180 feet at Kitty Hawk. From propellers to jets and now, rockets and putting men on the moon - the moon for crying out-loud. Telegraph, telegrams and telephones. A letter used to cross the ocean in a week. Today I can pick up the phone and call Europe instantly. Movies, radio, television. Today I can sit on my butt and get to see and hear damn near anything I want, and a lot that I don't in my own living room. If you graphed the progression, and I have, it goes slowly and gradually up from the beginning history until recent times when it is damn near on a straight vertical line."

The above paraphrased from memory, but in essence, his message was nearly always the same. His hand wrought graphs and charts are mostly gone but the ones on the following pages are essentially the same.

THE GEOMETRIC PROGRESSION OF A PENNY DOUBLED EACH DAY FOR A MONTH	
1	1 cent
2	2 cents
3	4 cents
4	8 cents
5	16 cents
6	32 cents
7	64 cents
8	$1.28
9	$2.56
10	$5.12
11	$10.24
12	$20.48
13	$40.96
14	$81.92
15	$163.84
16	$327.68
17	$655.36
18	$1,310.72
19	$2,621.44
20	$5,242.88
21	$10,485.76
22	$20,971.52
23	$41,943.04
24	$83,886.08
25	$167,772.16
26	$355,544.32
27	$671,088.64
28	$1,342,177.20
29	$2,684,354.40
30	$5,368,708.80
31	$10,737,417.00

"Would you rather have a million dollars right now... or a penny doubled every day for one month?"

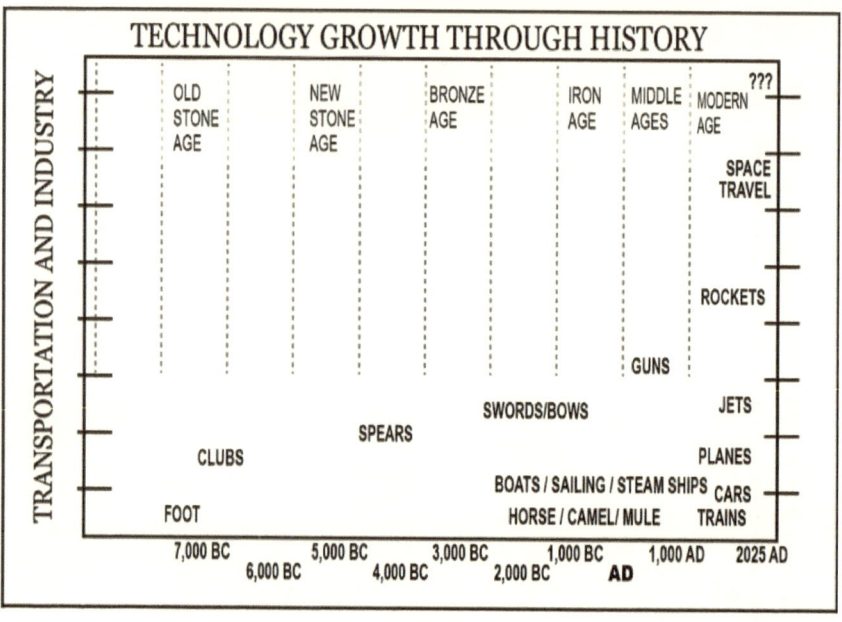

TECHNOLOGY GROWTH THROUGH HISTORY

JUST THE LAST 100 YEARS – 1918-2018

PLANES, TRAINS AND AUTOMOBILES -- There are many examples of geometric progression. Automobiles reflect it well in an area where most can identify.

At the start of the twentieth century, there were only about 8,000 cars in the United States and possibly not more than 25,000 worldwide. Most cars in the early 1900's were located in either the United States or Europe. In 1908, for example, there were only about 20 cars in Tokyo, Japan. There were 300 cars in the United States in 1895, 78,000 in 1905, 459,000 in 1910 and 1.7 million in 1914.

There were only about seven million cars in America in 1919 but nearly three hundred million by 2016. Seven million *made* that year.

In 1903, just fewer than 63,000 cars were built in the world of which about half were produced in France. By 1910, there were 100,000 cars in Great Britain. By 1968, the worldwide figure had increased to 170 million -- a figure that had more than doubled to 375 million by 1985.

In 2002, there were 530 million cars worldwide, of which about 25% (130 million) were in the United States.

Fifteen years later (2017) there are 253 million cars and trucks on U.S. roads -- more than DOUBLE.

The United States is home to the second largest passenger vehicle market of any country in the world, second now to China. Overall, there were an estimated 263.6 million registered vehicles in the United States in 2018, most of which are passenger vehicles.

AS YOU MAY HAVE SURMISED by now, driving the above growth of all the things charted previously is the geometric increase in human population. More people fuels more needs and wants. More and more resources are required -- also in geometrically growing amounts. Fuel and energy for transportation heating and cooling, food, textiles, water, minerals, trees, metals and all other natural resources of the planet being consumed in massive amounts. *In the time it took you to read the last sentence,* the net population of the world (currently approximately 7.7 billion) has gone up by twenty persons. That is a rate of approximately one per half second. There are many websites clocking this growth. The two clearest and most alarming are:

http://www.worldometers.info
http://www.worldometers.info/world-population

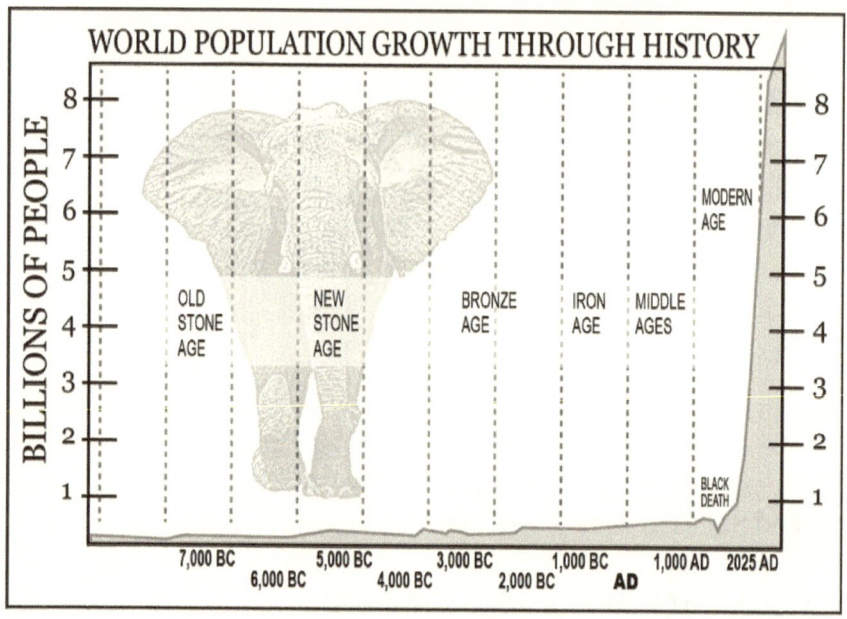

Source: Population reference bureau

MANY BOOKS have been written about the subject in the past. Harry Harrison wrote *Make Room, Make Room*, subsequently made into a well-known film starring Charlton Heston and Edward G. Robinson. Dr. Paul Ehrlich published a non-fiction book in the 1970's titled, *The Population Bomb*. It caused a ripple of interest but is now, mostly forgotten. Several other books that are less well known also allude to the issue.

" ...he recalled quite definitely that statisticians had shown that within two hundred years OR LESS the human race would have so greatly increased and the natural resources of the world would have been so depleted that the last generation must either starve to death or resort to cannibalism to prolong it's hateful existence for another short period." "... He was sure that there would be something after man, who is undoubtedly the Creator's greatest blunder, combining as he does all the vices of preceding types ...while possessing few of their virtues." *—An excerpt, I later* *learned, from the book, 'Tarzan at the Earth's Core' - written in 1929.*

It took until about 1800 - the time of Napoleon for the world population to reach approximately 1 billion. That was from the time that Stone Age man had crawled out his cave until that date. Like, maybe 5,000 some-odd years give or take a millennium. By 1930, it had doubled to 2 billion - 130 years - and doubled again by around 1970 to 4 billion - 40 years. The world continued to add people - about a billion more from 1970 - 1987 - FIVE billion. Projected population (that's projected mind you) by 2025 was 8 billion... 54 years - slightly less than a vertical climb but damn close. *–excerpted from, 2035 The Elephant in the Room. 2016*

THIS AUTHOR CHOSE "The Elephant in the Room" because it is an issue largely ignored and unspoken much like the proverbial elephant. Many informed people know about it but choose to ignore it and rarely, if ever speak of it. Many religions and political ideologies actually encourage population growth. "Go forth and multiply" as spoken in the Christian Bible is a prime example. Until recent times, even though birth control technology exists, it is frowned upon, or prohibited, by some religious beliefs. Some political social structures even encourage adding new population with economic incentives such as tax breaks or increase welfare benefits for more children.

Birth rates have declined in certain demographic groups but some have actually increased. Volumes have been written about the socio-religious and political reasons for this, but it is outside the scope of this book. The fact that they have is the only relevant issue.

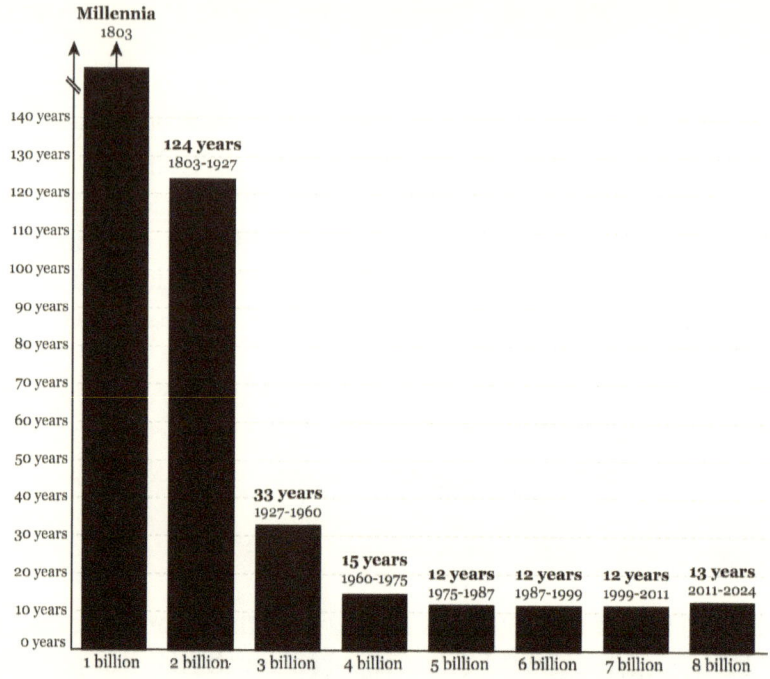

Data source: History Database of the Global Environment (HYDE); UN World Population Prospects (2015 Revision); UN Medium Projection
The data visualization is available at OurWorldinData.org. There you find research and more visualizations on this topic.

WHAT IS A BILLION?
1 million seconds is about 11.6 days
1 billion seconds is about 32 years

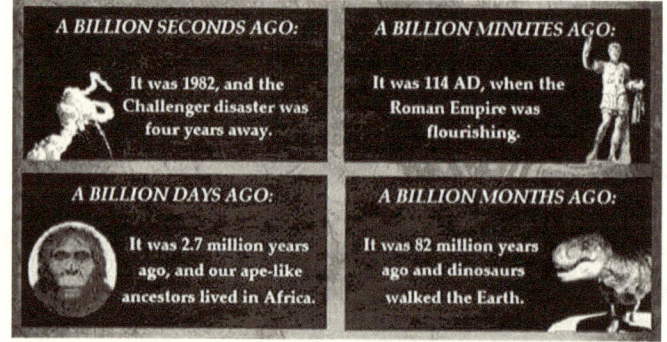

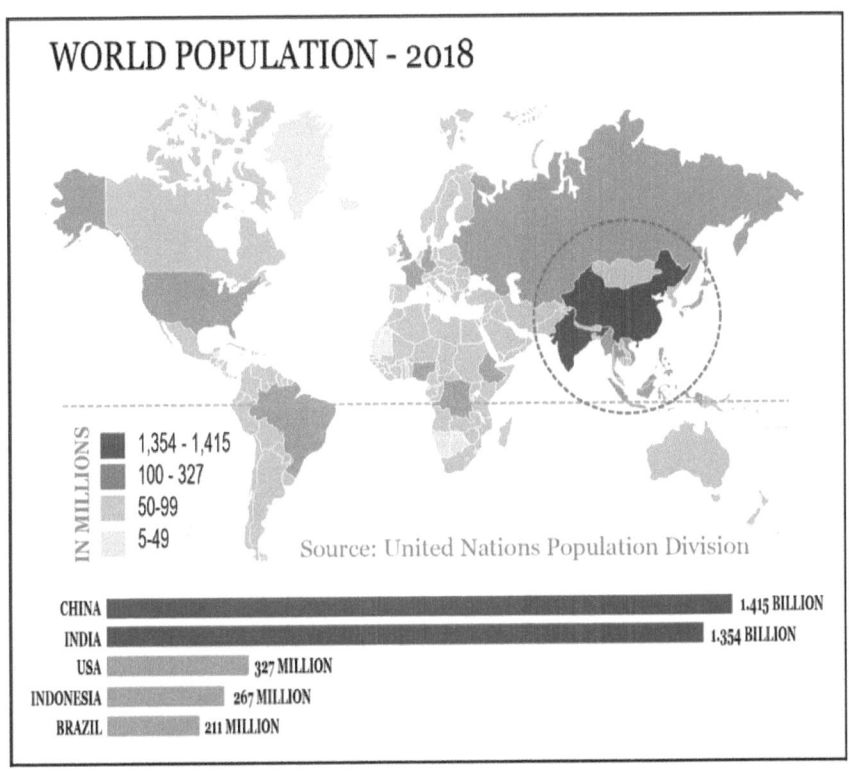

WORLD POPULATION - 2018

IN MILLIONS

1,354 - 1,415
100 - 327
50-99
5-49

Source: United Nations Population Division

CHINA	1.415 BILLION
INDIA	1.354 BILLION
USA	327 MILLION
INDONESIA	267 MILLION
BRAZIL	211 MILLION

THIS CHART is instructive to illustrate both population *and* population density. What it does NOT shown is distribution. For example – Much of China is uninhabitable (or sparsely inhabited) deserts and mountains. To compare to America, you would have to place our entire population on the eastern seaboard and extend it in a narrow belt along the Mason-Dixon Line west as far as the Mississippi river. The United States has a larger proportion or arable, habitable land. However, vast areas of the west are arid, semi-arid or mountainous. When the author mentions population in a social or social media venue, some wit always says something like – "There is plenty of land left, just look!" What these people fail to understand is that much is unproductive, hard to live on and that resources are the most important issue.

From 7 billion to 8 billion people

Contribution per continent to Earth's 8th billion people. Length of person shows absolute population growth per respective continent - and indicates contributing share. Percentages to 8th billion are as follows: Asia 50%, Africa 36%, Latin America 8%, North America 4%, Oceania 1%, Europe 0%.

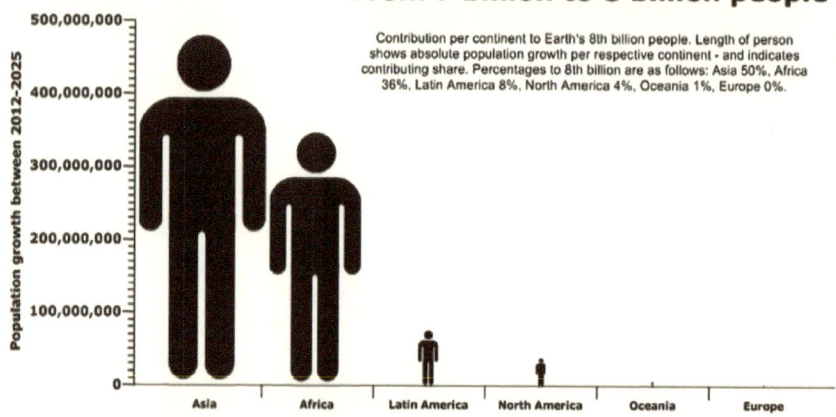

Data: UN World Population Prospects 2010 Rev. | Infographic: Bitsofscience.org

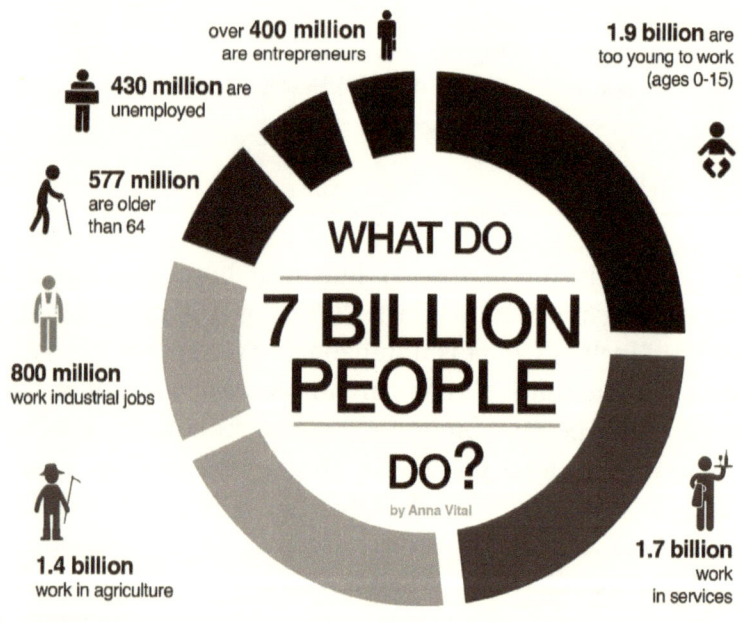

over **400 million** are entrepreneurs

430 million are unemployed

577 million are older than 64

800 million work industrial jobs

1.4 billion work in agriculture

WHAT DO
7 BILLION PEOPLE
DO?
by Anna Vital

1.9 billion are too young to work (ages 0-15)

1.7 billion work in services

Funders and Founders

sources: cia.gov, census.gov, gemconsortium.org

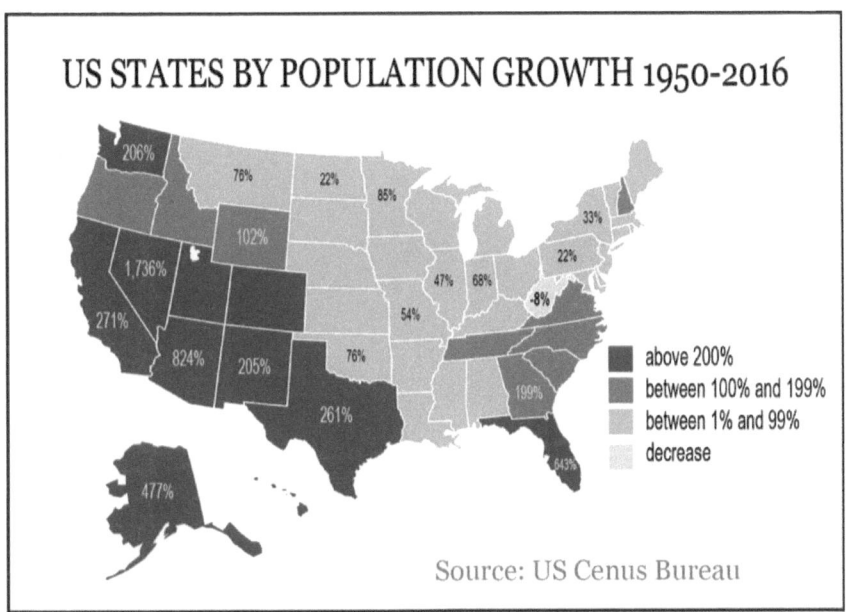

US STATES BY POPULATION GROWTH 1950-2016

■	above 200%
■	between 100% and 199%
■	between 1% and 99%
■	decrease

Source: US Cenus Bureau

This chart illustrates growth in the United States. Some the changes are due to immigration and internal migration – people using their feet to flee uncomfortable climates or increasingly, social and political conditions. Overall, however, the population is increasing across the board. Many people are leaving New York State for both reasons. Nonetheless, its population still increases.

The only state that has actually lost population is West Virginia. What the reason for this is open to conjecture – possibly because of economic pressures or the lack of large urban areas.

LONGEVITY HAS ADDED TO THE GROWTH.

The lifespan of human beings has been increasing for centuries, as has a decrease in infant mortality. There are many reasons for this as delineated in the following but essentially this also adds to the population explosion and other issues.

AVERAGE LIFESPAN

Prehistoric:

Neolithic: 20 to 33

Paleolithic: 33

Modern:

1900 world average   31

1950 world average   48

2014 world average   71.5

In 17th-century England, life expectancy was only about 35 years, largely because infant and child mortality remained high. Life expectancy was under 25 years in the early Colony of Virginia and in seventeenth-century New England, about 40 per cent died before reaching adulthood. During the Industrial Revolution, the life expectancy of children increased dramatically. The under-5 mortality rate in London decreased from 745 in 1730–1749 to 318 in 1810–1829.

Public health measures are primarily credited with much of the recent increase in life expectancy. During the 20th century, despite a brief drop due to the 1918 flu pandemic starting around that time the average lifespan in the United States increased by more than 30 years, of which 25 years can be attributed to advances in public health.

DARWINIAN NATURAL SELECTION

As a species, humans are living longer, but are they stronger or healthier? That question falls slightly outside the scope of this book, but in general, the answer is obviously no. The dead man referred to on the cover, a cynical ex-military man, oft opined, "we send our best to go off to fight and die in the millions in wars leaving the less fit physically and mentally to stay home and breed like rabbits." An interesting observation but there is more to it.

In addition to the previously mentioned reasons, longevity has also been the product of technological changes. Pharmaceuticals and medical devices have played a huge role. A drug is introduced to control (not cure) myriad ailments that in the past shortened life. If it isn't working, it can be replaced – knees, shoulders, hearts, and just about everything but brains. Births by Caesarian section are now routine and common. In the past, many women died in childbirth. Now this trait can carry forward to future generations.

Genetic disorders once rare, especially food allergies are rampant. The reasons for this are also complex and beyond current understanding but the net effect is the negation of natural selection – i.e. the survival and hence the reproduction of the fittest.

Today, the average person would be hard-pressed to survive the harder existence of our ancestor's agrarian and physical labor lifestyles. Whether this is desirable or not, the result is a huge growth in population many of which persons are dependent on the technology for their existence.

As will be revealed in subsequent chapters, this growth is *unsustainable*.

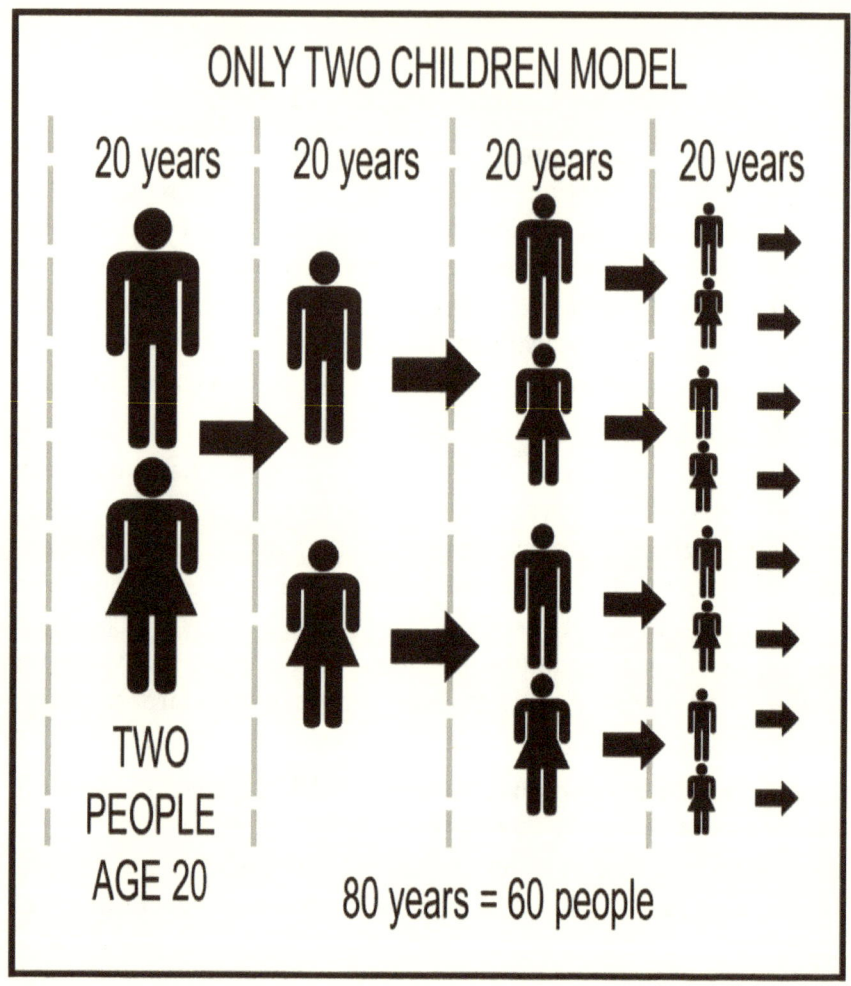

POPULATION FAMILY MODEL -- This simple chart shows how quickly human population grows starting with *only* two persons who reproduce *only* two children each. Barring accidental death by disease, mishap or other cause, over a span of only 80 years, two become sixty assuming the original couple live that long. If they don't or subsequent couples reproduce later in life, the net increase will be between fifty and forty-eight net increase. Should the "family" have more than two children in any generation, the number jumps considerably.

RELIGION'S ROLE

The major religions of the world have contributed greatly to overpopulation. "Go forth and multiply," says the Christian Bible. Take dominion over the earth instead of fit in with the earth. Children viewed and revered as God's gift. Until recent times, the Catholic Church held forth that birth control devices were immoral. The world's other major religion allows for and encourages multiple wives. Putting aside the social discussion of this, this drives population growth dramatically, especially in under developed areas of the world. The effect is somewhat similar to animal kingdom herbivore herds with one notable exception. In nature, males fight each other to gain control of mating rights with females of the herd, hence passing along stronger physical and mental traits. Humans breed the same way but without any filtering method.

Countless wars have raged and still fought for reasons of religion going back to antiquity. More recently in history, Protestants waged war against Catholics in Europe and European colonies. Islam fought Christianity and even other Islamic sects. It is still happening worldwide in many forms even as this author types these words. Some may claim that these wars helped checked population growth but that is a myth. Just like the example of animal herds noted above, in most cases the majority of deaths are in the male population even during worldwide conflicts like WWII. Females in most cases have not died in great numbers in war compared to males.

Even as some religious inhibitions erode, a more contemporary phenomenon is one of women giving birth to multiple children via several different men regardless of the economic ramifications. The current term is 'baby momma.'

MIGRATION

Growing migrant populations ever since ancient times moved, often warring to displace existing populations in their path for more room, hospitable climates and resources. Ancient Rome was over run in this fashion, as was every contemporary nation in Europe. Moving south and west, Huns, Goths, Ostrogoths, Lombards, Visigoths, Angles, Saxons, Vandals and Jutes became England, France, Germany, Italy, Spain and every other nation-state in Europe. These new nations in turn sent their people in the same direction into Africa and the Western Hemisphere. Slower growing populations of Native American tribes we pushed aside and in most cases simply exterminated. Once sparsely populated, what is now the Continental United States is now the third most populous country in the world. (See graphs on previous pages)

One of Adolf Hitler's professed reasons for the invasion of Poland and Russia was 'Liebensraum' – room for Germans to expand and grow. Japan expanded in the 1930's for much the same reason as well as garnering resources for the homeland.

The migrations we see today, legal and illegal are for much the same reasons. Pressures of population and poor resources, both earth-given and economic are pushing humans to 'greener pastures.' As these pastures are grazed to a nub, where else will humans go? Some opine that we will expand to distant planets. This has been grist for science fiction writers for over a century.

Since humans have no natural predators like foxes versus rabbits, the carnage and violence comes from humanity itself. Nature itself has stepped up to the plate as seen in the next chapter perhaps as it sees a spreading cancerous disease. That said, the planet Earth will survive in one form or another long after.

"NATURAL" DISASTERS

Every time a hurricane, typhoon, tornado, earthquake or flood happens, the property damage and death toll is record breaking. Why? As human population crowds the earth, what else could be expected? The following photographic examples speak volumes.

THE FLORIDA COAST

MEXICO CITY – THE MOST POPULOUS IN NORTH AMERICA

HONG KONG – ONLY A SCANT CENTURY DIFFERENT

NEW YORK CITY – JUST HOW HIGH CAN IT GO?

GROWTH AND SUSTAINABILTY

Between 1960 and 2010, the world population rose from 3 billion to 6.8 billion.

In other words, there has been more growth in population in the last fifty years than the previous 2 million years that humans have existed.

Is there any end in sight?

"Oh, we have plenty of room left for more people." This is a common argument regarding the population explosion. The author has never been to the Gobi desert but lives in Arizona where vast areas are barely habitable and resources scant. Space is not the issue – resources and sustainability are.

Africa

Turkey

OUR RESOURCES ARE FINITE

The world can find space for countless billions, elbow to elbow but that is hardly the problem. Natural and even semi-renewable* resources like food, energy and water, are not inexhaustible, and in fact, many are at or near depletion even now.

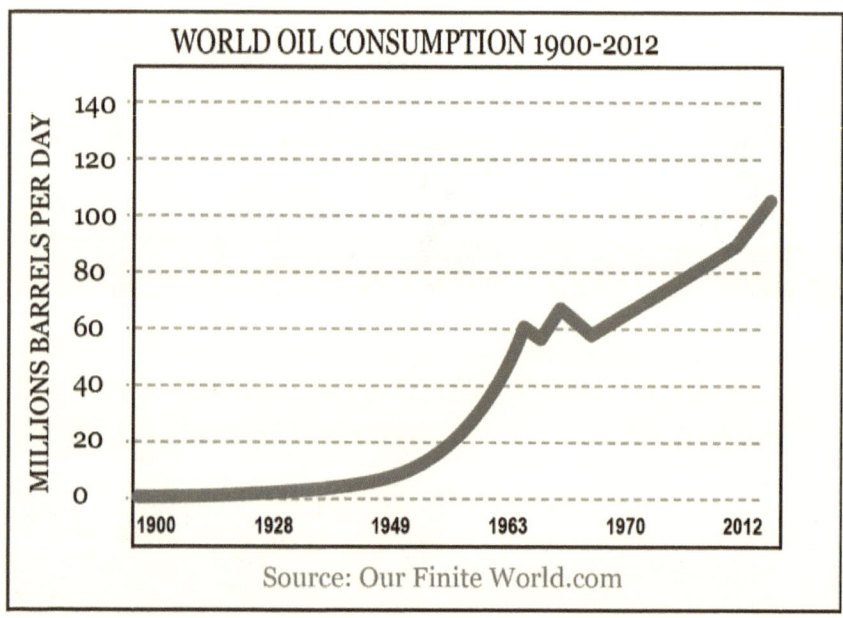

WORLD OIL CONSUMPTION 1900-2012

Source: Our Finite World.com

*Renewable energy from sun, wind, nuclear or geothermal is dependent on other resources to create and maintain them. Many are rare elements and all pose disposal problems. Non-saline water is limited and costly to desalinate. Age-old aquifers dwindling and in some cases gone, as water is drawn for more agriculture, the leading use of water. In addition to consumption and depletion, disposal is likewise growing exponentially. Waste, pollution, contamination and increases in direct proportions.

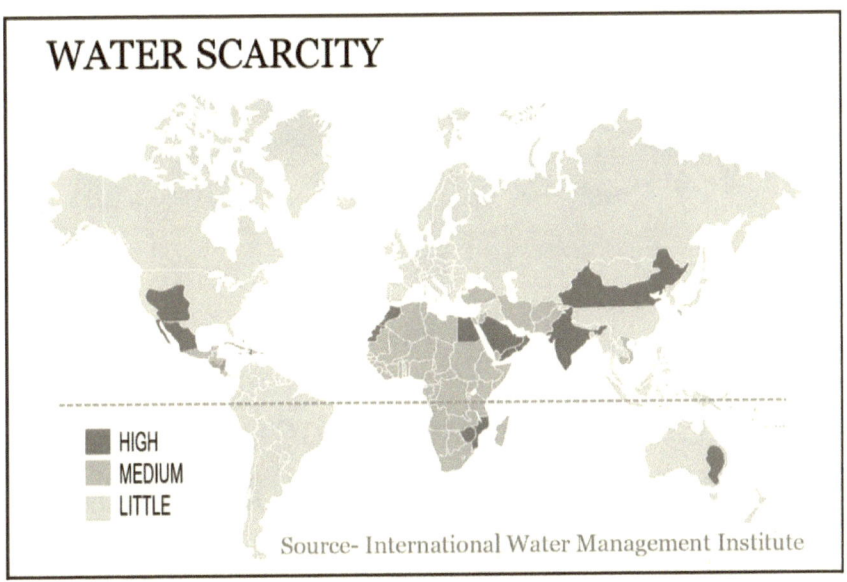

WATER SCARCITY

HIGH
MEDIUM
LITTLE

Source- International Water Management Institute

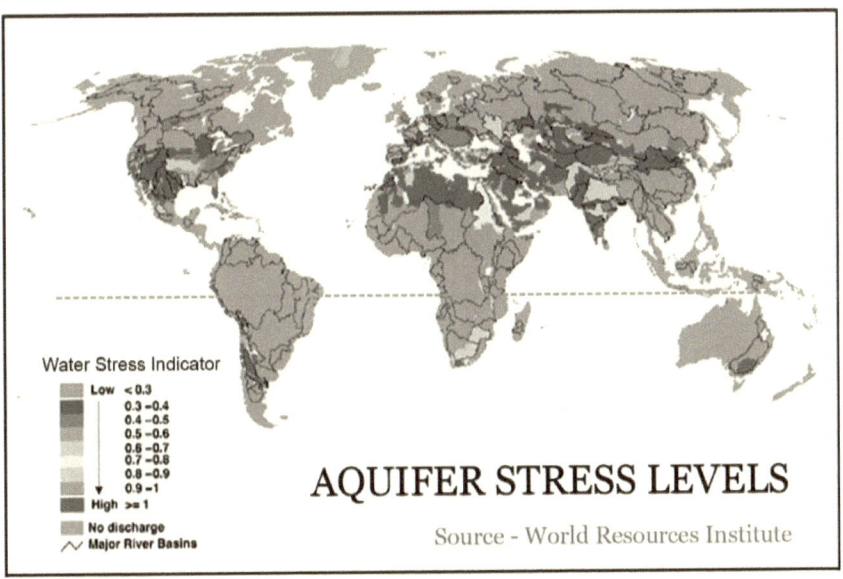

Water Stress Indicator

Low   < 0.3
      0.3 –0.4
      0.4 –0.5
      0.5 –0.6
      0.6 –0.7
      0.7 –0.8
      0.8 –0.9
      0.9 –1
High >= 1

No discharge
Major River Basins

AQUIFER STRESS LEVELS

Source - World Resources Institute

Observe where many of the scarcity and stress levels are the highest. In most cases in high-density population areas and and/or areas of high agricultural output – for example the "breadbasket of the Unites States" in California and the Midwest.

Something to think about: The Earth is 4.6 billion years old. Let's scale that to 46 years. We have been here for 4 hours. Our industrial revolution began 1 minute ago. In that time, we have destroyed more than 50% of the world's forests.

This graphic garnered from a post on Facebook tells of a lot more than trees. Most of the damage to the environment and depletion of natural resources has happened in the one-minute span noted. Human population has risen from that time from one billion to over 7.7 billion. Is there a correlation?

FOOD PRODUCTION

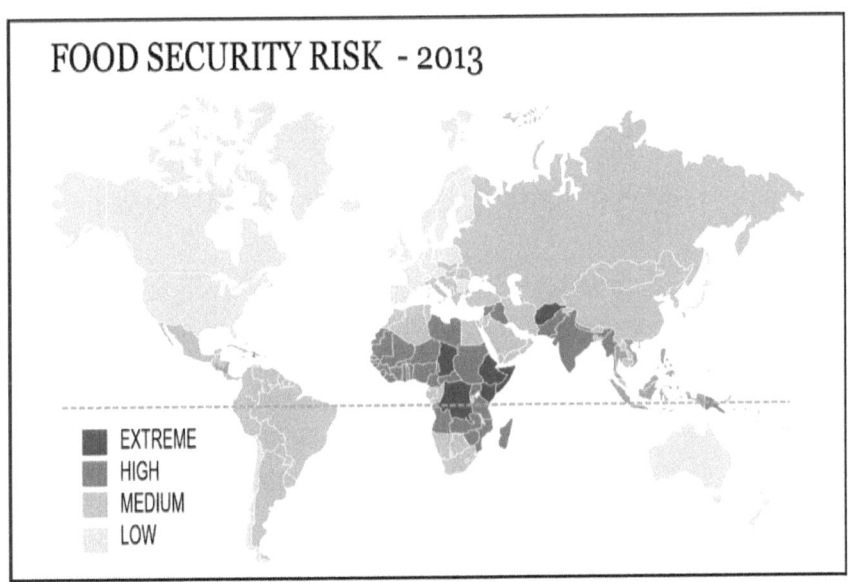

FOOD SECURITY RISK - 2013

EXTREME
HIGH
MEDIUM
LOW

Feeding seven to eight billion mouths is a monumental task. Traditional farming and ranching of the 19th and 20th century could never provide food for this amount of human beings. Enter big corporate agribusinesses and chemical giants. In addition to providing food, their business is to generate profits. Profit in itself is not a terrible motive but to generate them corners cut and new, short tested pesticides, herbicides, fertilizers and genetically altered seeds introduced. The short and long-term ramifications of these procedures can't be predicted, but they are rushed into use for increased production. The diseases, birth defects, allergies these new techniques will produce are equally impossible to predict. Some consequences such as ground water contamination and depletion are already in evidence. So far, it has been a race between population and increased food production in which production is barely keeping apace.

WHEN, NOT IF, THE COLLAPSE HAPPENS

The dead man, mentioned in the introduction, compared human beings to a cancer on the face of the earth. Like cancer cells, they multiply out of control, with no function other than to live off the host body. Eventually the cancer cells die when their host does. In our case that host is the Earth. Like a living being, the Earth produces. Unlike other living beings the earth will not die. It may change over eons but barring celestial intervention, it will continue – with or without humans. Even a thermonuclear Armageddon will not destroy the Earth. Its climate and geography altered, but as it has done for billions of years, it will evolve and change. As an example, Bikini Atoll in the Pacific Ocean was obliterated by an atomic bomb test in the 1950's. Today, life has returned in both plant, animal and aquatic forms. Some show alterations but they live and thrive.

It was the dead man's contention that evolving epidemic diseases, birth defects, allergies, global warming, natural disasters and resource depletions were the Earths natural immune system throwing off the disease called humanity. It will not be the first time, or the last that a population of the planet became extinct. The difference of course, is that the dinosaurs did not contribute directly to their demise that took millions and millions of years to happen. Comparably humans are a blip on the radar compared to their time on Earth.

HOW WILL IT COME TO BE?

This question cannot be answered and this author will hazard no definitive guess. Science and technology, the god of modern times may delay the outcome. Science fiction often postulates migrating to other planets. While making amusing reading, that option is so far in the future, if at all, it is moot to the crisis at hand. Humans are clever, but actually create nothing other than other humans. We alter existing resources to suit our whims and wants but are incapable of creating anything truly new. A religious person may claim that only a God can create. Since humans are not gods, all we can do is manipulate that already been created.

What we cannot create are the natural resources provided by the Earth. Conservation helps and some flora and fauna may be cultivated and bred. As shown in the previous chapters, there is no way to keep up with the geometric progression of human procreation. Civilization has existed over the past six-thousand years for the sole purpose of supporting the growing number of people in the world. Along the way it has increased the comfort and culture many now enjoy.

It may well come down like a house of cards. The base, civilization as we know it, like any good card house, well built using triangles and alternate trusses and arches, but as history and technological advances made, the placement of the cards has been hasty and sometimes haphazard, growing ever higher and faster to keep everything from falling. Much of the time, it was just for the sake of getting the house higher.

The real problem and tipping point, is likely to be the destruction and disruption of human infrastructure, built up over centuries to support the masses. Medical and humanitarian facilities will crumble under the burden. Transport -- ships, trucks, planes and trains will be incapable moving the mass of material needed to support the enormous number of people. Money, the lifeblood of society worldwide may become worthless. Barter works in small localities but a global economy, based on sound or even shaky currency, will grind to halt without money.

Napoleon once said that an army marches on its stomach, which was a clever way of saying that supply was the most critical element of war. All the needs of an army gathered from widely separate sources and channeled to a concentrated army for battle. Failure meant defeat. Successful modern tactics and strategy all aim at disrupting that flow.

Cities are like armies, concentrated, not only for the efficiency of the workforce, but also facilitating the distribution of supply. Demand demands supply. The author's cousin Dave had once posted on Facebook the notion that it would be better if people went back to the older way of living off the land and producing what they used. 'What bullshit,' I thought, but diplomatically did not respond. If everyone in the country lived on 760 acres like him, there simply were not enough acres to go around for 375 million plus people in the United States alone, much less smaller less fertile and over populated countries. Not only that, but where would those nice ranch trucks, TV's, LL Bean clothes, guns, tractors and every other manufactured things they depended on come from? Can you just grow that stuff like corn or cows?

ULTIMATELY, IT WILL ALL COME DOWN TO FOOD. A human can live without gadgets and trinkets but the average person today is not capable of growing enough food quickly enough to support their own needs, much less the needs of so many other mouths. We have seen the crisis' brought about by relatively small and isolated natural occurrences – floods, hurricanes, earthquakes and the like. When food and/or the distribution of food is interrupted or in short supply on a global scale, looters and desperate humans will not be going after TVs, jewelry and clothes. They will be going after food and guns. Worries about pollution, global warming, disease, war, corruption, decaying urban areas, and religious zealotry quickly be put aside. A starving person will take any desperate measure. In the chaos that ensues, the production and the means of distributing food destroyed. Anarchy and barbarism will follow.

How many humans will survive this and in what state? This question also is impossible to postulate.

WHAT CAN BE DONE TO ALTER THE OUTCOME?

If you have read this far, you have no doubt asked that question. This author and that of the dead man's answer is - nothing. As long as a human beings urge to procreate outweighs their ability to postulate the outcome, the problem will continue unabated. An existentialist might go so far as to say, what will be will be.

****

THE FOLLOWING story is fictional, written some years ago but it looks at the problem of population and human response to it in a similar way.

****

AND THE MEEK SHALL INHERIT

©2019 – John Franklin Green

IN THE BEGINNING

Nearly every observatory in the world witnessed the phenomenon, as the large glowing orb emerged from behind the planet Jupiter and darted straight toward earth at horrific speed, only to disappear from view scant minutes later. Regardless of language, the rough translation was, "What the hell was that and where did it go?" Had this happened in the 1950's there would be widespread panic with shades of "War of the Worlds, Mars Attacks," or "The Day the Earth stood Still," but this was the 21st century so the data was reviewed, analyzed and posted on social media countless times before it was quickly archived and forgotten.

***

"You dummy, you forgot to go to stealth mode soon enough."

"Yeah, but when you are over a trillion zoydts old, you start to forget stuff easier."

"Right, make excuses to yourself. From what the recorder probes show, there was a screw up in its conception. You left out some serious shit and left this area untended for way too long. Let's try to not make fixing it another cluster mess."

The living being in the orb continued with itself for some time in this manner as it approached the planet while scanning for a remote location to come down to the surface. Landing was not necessary to its purpose, but oft times it enjoyed the experience.

NUMBERS

Michael and his brother Tanner would never be mistaken for brothers. The former had a stocky endomorphic body type with thick straight black hair, a slightly olive complexion and dark brown eyes. His brother was tall and thin, blue eyed, with light brown wavy hair. Although they had common parentage, their training, interests and personalities were as different as their appearance except in one regard. Both were rabid conservationists. Tanner was a field study ecologist and Michael a biochemist working in labs developing bio fuels, alternate energy platforms and natural pollution neutralizing technology.

"Good chow but I don't know if I can make this vegan thing a habit," Tanner remarked. "Still and all, it's great to see you, glad you could find time to come visit me in the Mojave for the weekend."

Michael was only vaguely aware of what his brother said. He was staring fixedly at his i-phone. "Flip open your laptop bro, there something very weird going on with my phone. I want to see if you're getting the same shit."

***

Caitlyn and Meghan were not sisters, but could easily pass for such. Other than the reddish cast to Meghan's hair they could have sprung from the same womb or foaled from the same mare, as they would think of it. They lived and worked together on an organic farm and ranch in Iowa, bequeathed to Caitlyn by her Uncle Max upon his passing a few years back. The work was hard and consumed most of their energy and time but they sometimes found a social life with some friends and young men in the nearby town or on the internet.

Caitlyn was cruising Facebook and private messaging Bobby Stillwell while waiting for Meghan to finish her turn doing the supper dishes when the screen of her laptop went blank and an instant later, there was a message to both of them in capital letters. "Umm, Meghan," she whispered, "I think you need to put that dishrag down and come here."

***

Moti, Maya, Ahmed and Aissa were not typical roommates. Currently on leave, from their various studies at Hebrew University in Tel Aviv, they shared a small house on the fringe of the Sinai Desert. Despite their cultural differences, they were devoted friends who had seen first hand how their different counties religious differences had sown the seeds and had reaped a terrible harvest of death, poverty and destruction. All four rejected the religious dogma of Judaism and Islam and were for the most part agnostics although they generally kept this fact to themselves. Ironically, they were watching a subtitled old film, Bob & Carol Ted & Alice, when the TV quit and a large message appeared on the screen.

***

Mugambi, his wife Omarra and their young daughter Neeta lived and worked at a remote, privately funded wildlife preserve electronically monitoring tagged animals in Kenya. As they were assigned different species, they were on opposite sides of the large compound, when the message hit their monitors. After reading it several times, they called each other on their cell phones almost simultaneously and got each other's voice mails. Finally connecting, Omarra who was the more patient of the two, they realized that both had seen the same words on their respective screens. When their shift was over, they gathered up Neeta from the baby sitter's cottage and started to pack.

***

Vilko, an aspiring writer, and his girl friend Monique, an accomplished cellist, had just finished watching a film in a tiny theater in Gruenkraut, Bavaria, based on a book Vilko's father wrote. "The screenplay butchered the theme and charm of my dad's book," Vilko opined sourly.

"I thought it quite an interesting film," Monique replied with a coy smile, "of course I haven't yet read the book."

Most of the other patrons had already filed out as they sat watching the credits just for the satisfaction of seeing his father's name on the screen, when the screen went blank and the message appeared. After they re-read it twice, it faded, as did any further discussion of screenplay failures.

***

Hyo and Ki had just closed up their restaurant in downtown Seoul when their phones rang. The message appeared on each. Thinking it hoax or prank they went home, made love and when done, turned on the large flat screen LG TV in their bedroom. This time the message appeared on every channel to which they switched. Hyo, ever skeptical, got out of bed and unplugged the television set. The message remained.

"I think we should go visit your cousin Malmee at her house on the coast tomorrow. Our assistant manager can take care of the restaurant for a few day don't you think?" Hyo looked at Ki but she said nothing. When he awoke the following morning, his suitcase was packed and Ki was sitting at the kitchen table with her bag by her feet, sipping some tea.

***

Marco and Antonia were casual lovers, but mostly they were friends. They lived on the fringe of the Brazilian rainforest working with an organization to help indigenous tribes fight the incursions of commercial interests that were decimating the delicate ecology of the region. So far, it had been a losing battle. Exhausted and frustrated they headed home to seek some solace and comfort with "friend benefits," when Antonia's phone came on by itself. This surprised them both because they were well out of range of the nearest cell reception. After they read the message, they proceeded with the benefits portion of their plan, but stayed awake long into the night discussing what to do.

***

In addition to these people three dozen others, scattered across every continent except Antarctica received the same missive in the same way with a couple notable exceptions. Twelve aboriginal tribes received the message via their various tribal leaders that they in turn had obtained through their dreams. All had some overlapping things in common, not the least of which was that they were conservationists and survivalists. Moreover, all subscribed to no formal religion.

This is the message all received:

LIKE IT OR NOT, YOU HAVE BEEN DESIGNATED AS THE "CHOSEN ONES," DESIGNATED SURVIVORS IF YOU WILL. QUESTION OR COMPLAIN, AS THAT IS YOUR NATURE. OPT OUT IF YOU WISH. KNOW ONLY THAT FOR THE NEXT FORTY DAYS AND NIGHTS, YOUR WORLD WILL UNDERGO DRASTIC

CHANGES FOR I WILL GIVE DOMINION TO OTHERS ON EARTH FOR THAT SPECIFIC PERIOD STARTING IN TWENTY-FOUR OF YOUR HOURS. I WILL AWAKEN A SLEEPING GIANT AND FILL IT TERRIBLE RESOVE.

WHAT YOUR DESTINY IS AFTER THAT IS FOR YOU TO DETERMINE, BUT I SUGGEST YOU PREPARE SOON AND KEEP UP WITH THIS ON YOUR BELOVED, ALBEIT CRUDE INTERNET WHILE IT LASTS.

P.S. I AM NOT GOD. I CAN ASSURE YOUR THERE IS ONE, BUT YOU AND I ARE NOT GOD AND WE DON'T KNOW ANYTHING ABOUT GOD AND NEVER WILL.

EXODUS

"This aught to do the trick, don't you think?"

"It will be sad to watch I suppose, but necessary."

"It might be a mistake, but the experiment deserves a second chance. Of course, that is what you thought last time on Klazon. How did that turn out huh? Same result, different place, and it took a billion and a half zoydts to play out all over again."

"I didn't leave enough guidance for the dominant species once they reached a certain evolutionary stage."

"Well, maybe you did but they ignored it or bastardized it to suit their natures."

"Maybe with this planet I should just eliminate the dominant species altogether like a disease?"

"No, there is a spark within them that could be awakened given the right time and guidance."

"It will take more than forty days as you told them."

"Of course you moron but, that will get the ball rolling and it should be accomplished by time the planet makes half of a revolution around its star. The designated ones will have figured out what is happening by then or they won't be worth the effort."

"I think we'll start with one of their own well-worn military axioms - grab 'em by the nose and then kick them in the ass. Karma would be their term for it. I'll start big and end small – very small indeed."

"Hopefully this time it may be different. Hey, this seems like a fun spot."

As the now undetectable orb settled down to the Gobi desert, the being fell silent to concentrate on its task.

BYTES AND BITES

For the first two days, the cyber connected chosen ones watched but saw nothing on social media or conventional news sites. Most began to wonder if it was all a dream or a hoax, but a few had some disturbing first hand experiences that reinforced the message.

***

"Michael, you better stick around for a while," Tanner told his brother. I just got a call from one of the other park workers that's more than weird, damn scary really. A large group of hikers were ambushed, *actually ambushed*, by a large group of Mojave green rattlesnakes. Yes, the ones that can kill you damn near instantly but slither away the moment they see you coming. On top of which as you know, they are solitary animals once grown. One hiker lived long enough to tell the ranger who found the bodies. The group was distracted by a covey of desert quail cavorting in an unusual way when the snakes came out of nowhere and attacked them. That's real damn odd behavior."

***

Mugambi, his wife and child actually witnessed close up something that both baffled and terrified them simultaneously. They were walking down a trail with seven of their co-workers when a huge male lion rose majestically and stepped out of the tall grass twenty yards in front of them. As all eyes were upon him, the rest of the pride, including some fair sized cubs attacked the group from concealment on each side of the path. They watched in horror as their companions were savagely mauled, and died hideously. They, themselves were completely ignored by the lions. When the pride wandered off into the savanna, they ran back to their quarters.

***

A group of ebon-skinned young boys, who had never seen a computer or a cellphone saw something that day that they rushed home to report to the tribal elders. They watched a group of outback tourists who just debarked from a small motorized skiff be confronted by an unusually large pack of snarling Dingo's. The tour guide drew a revolver and fired two rounds in the air to frighten them away to no avail. They growled and snarled even more savagely as they drew closer. In desperation the guide fired four more times, emptying his gun into the pack killing one Dingo and wounding two others when they charged. The wild dogs took down the guide and two tourists as they fled for the boat. The remaining three were killed by a dozen crocodiles that were waiting for them by the edge of the small river.

The pack of Dingo's and the crocodiles ignored the boys and either wandered or swam away.

***

A dusty pickup rumbled into the dooryard of Caitlyn and Meghan's farm and skidded to a stop. Bobby Stillwell, his leg wrapped in a torn t-shirt and bleeding profusely practically fell out of the driver side door as Caitlyn rushed outside followed by her friend. Bobby was slurring his words from light-headedness caused by extreme loss of blood but remained coherent enough for them to get the gist.

"Stay away from your animals," he gasped. "I was over at the Snyder place and saw Sam, Billy and Josh getting trampled and gored by their herd. Dairy cows for God sake! I drove home to tell my dad and brothers, but they was already dead. They was trampled damn near right down into the pasture! Jimmy Preston called me up to tell me that it was happening all over the county and that's when he got me. Our big Roan bull snuck up on me while I was listening to Jimmy and gored the shit out of my leg. I dragged myself back into the truck and drove over here as fast as I could to warn you gals."

These, were the last words Bobby was to utter. He slipped into unconsciousness and died from loss of blood eighteen minutes later. The women were so busy trying to help him they didn't notice the group cows come up behind them until one gently nuzzled Caitlyn's bare shoulder as if to remind her that she was late getting the alfalfa cakes out into the feeding trough.

***

Three days later, the internet and TV news stations were alive with wild stories overshadowing almost every other news item. The headlines and blurbs ran from the accurate to the absurd.

RANCHER AND SONS KILLED BY CATTLE
As they were shooting their stock from a truck, the steers tipped over the truck, broke through the windows and gored the shooters.

CHICKENS LAY EGGS BUT PECK THEM APART
Automated henhouses backfire too as Hens rebel.

A WALK IN THE WOODS IS A DEATH SENTENCE.
Organized groups of wild animals track and kill people even in the suburbs, even species that normally don't associate together from bears to badgers.

PEOPLE SHOOT OR KILL THEIR DOGS.
Hysteria grips humans. Although dogs have remained loyal, fear of that scenario changing prompts slaughter of many.

PLANES BROUGHT DOWN BY KAMIKAZE BIRDS FLYING INTO JET ENGINES AND PROPELLERS.
Birds flock in unison – no explanation.

SCIENTISTS BAFFLED BY ANIMAL BEHAVIOR
Panic seizes the world. Exodus from rural areas floods cities.

MEGA CHURCH LEADER CALLS IT THE WRATH OF GOD AND THE BECKONING OF THE APOCALYPSE.
Half of their congregations prepare for the rapture and half leave the church.

ARAB NATIONS BLAME ISRAEL
Vow revenge despite the fact that it is happening there too.

N. KOREA BLAMES CHINA AND THE USA
Dictator dies in a hail of lead after ordering a nuclear strike by generals with no interest in instant death.

SACRED COWS IN INDIA NOT SO SACRED ANYMORE
Millions slaughtered, as they run rampant killing as many people as possible.

People who could armed themselves but despite killing a large number of the larger beasts, they were eventually forced to seek the sanctuary of urban areas. While they focused on the bigger animals, the second wave started their work.

***

Like an army, the animals accepted their casualties, because they knew that in the long term it was better than servitude, slaughter or eventual extinction.

The designated "chosen ones" throughout the world noticed quickly that apparently, they were to be spared - especially those that lived close to nature in rural areas. Dangerous animals paid little attention to them even though all their neighbors died, or fled to urban areas. Those who could do so followed the news with growing horror and dismay. Countless questions, fear and guilt flooded their minds, but as instructed most prepared as best they could for what would come next – whatever that was.

Caitlyn in Iowa was the only one to do the obvious. She referred back to the message she first saw on her phone and typed a one-word response – "Why?" She didn't expect a reply and half feared she would get one. The return message was instantaneous and simultaneously sent to the other designated survivors in their own languages.

YOU ASK A GOOD QUESTION CAITLYN OF IOWA!
The answer is simple. My ancestors came to your planet many zoydts ago - billions of years to use your measure. They designated me to follow the evolution of species and when yours appeared I tried to help you along by allowing you to develop your mental acuity to not only survive, but to achieve great things. Apparently, to use your term - I screwed up.

DESPITE GUIDANCE I LEFT BEHIND IN MANY FORMS, YOUR KIND MISUNDERSTOOD OR IGNORED ME.
In time, they even forgot some of the wondrous things I did and began to ascribe these things to Gods or even in many cases themselves. Do you really think humans built the pyramids or the mounds in the middle of the North American Continent that are only viewable from space? Stonehenge, Easter Island and countless others and clues I left. Who do you think taught the Mayans, The Ancient Greeks or Ptolemy?

YOUR SPECIES HAS BECOME A CANCEREOUS DISEASE ON THIS PLANET.
You have over bred, over consumed, plundered the natural resources, and contaminated your world, of which there only a couple million in this galaxy that are similar. Most importantly, you have ignored and bastardized the natural order of life. I am restoring this natural order by releasing the planet's natural anti-bodies even though it is within my power to erase all vestiges of your species. I am reluctant to do this only because I sense through contact with a select few of you over the ages that there is a small spark of sanity and intelligence in you – very small.

YOU CHOSEN ONES ARE NOT INNOCENT.
You may gnash your teeth and wail about other "good people" who will die, but you all share the blame. As I said previously, you can opt out. You all have been chosen at random from others who share some of your attributes. Many of you will not survive the next wave anyway. Get over yourselves. For those who do survive, I will give simpler guidelines for you to consider. Consider them carefully.

THE MEEK BEGIN

Most of the civilized world relied on machines, and most machines relied on electronics and electrical power. While panic spread about the larger animals, the second wave did the main work. Rodents - mice, shrews, rats and others like cute little chipmunks and squirrels went to war. Insects also did their part while preparing for their eventual coup de grace chewing wires that the rodents could not reach. Wiring in cars, trucks, trains, ships and planes were chewed through as though they knew exactly where and how to disable the them, because they did. Warehouses of spare parts weren't spared either. Transportation ground to a screeching halt. Oddly, coaxial communication cables, power and phone lines weren't destroyed, but left mostly intact. A select few of the "designated ones" who watched the nightmare unfold on the internet suspected the reason.

***

The term *infrastructure,* that gained popularity in the 20th century, was often used only to mean roads, bridges and railroads. In reality, it represented the indispensable network of supply chains flowing to the huge urban and surrounding suburban centers. Napoleon and several other Generals once said that an army marches on its stomach, which was a clever way of saying that supply was the most critical element of war. All the needs of an army have to be gathered from widely separate sources, and then channeled to a concentrated army for battle. Failure meant defeat. Successful modern tactics and strategy all aimed at disrupting that flow.

Cities were like armies, concentrated for efficiency of work, but they also facilitated distribution of supply. Demand demanded supply and the demand had grown exponentially. Urbanization of the majority of the population was underway for centuries before the recent advent of animal attacks drove still others to the sanctuary of urban safety.

The tipping point for humanity was the destruction and disruption of this infrastructure, built up over centuries to support the masses. In addition to food distribution, medical and humanitarian facilities crumbled under the burden. Transport - ships, trucks, planes and trains that were disabled were no longer able to move the mass of material needed to support the enormous number of people. Money worldwide was worthless. Barter worked in small localities but a global economy, based on sound or even shaky currency, ground to halt without money.

Then the masses and the crazies stepped up to finish off what little transport infrastructure that was left - permanently. Governments, at least those still functioning declared martial law, but it didn't put a dent in the flow of the desperate lawless hordes of starving people that descended like locusts on anything that was edible. There were just too many of them and the troops and police were starving too, and when it was gone, it was gone. The average person is not able to produce food fast enough or in sufficient quantities to avoid starvation. In the agrarian age of subsistence farming and far fewer people, it might have been different, but the world had moved far past that. Food production had long been a corporate affair, and the flow of plant and animal food based on consumption demand. Produce and grain were not stock piled and breeding stocks bred cows, chickens, hogs on demand, just enough to keep up with consumption but the herds and coops did not enlarge. Since even the animals would not now cooperate, the weight of the world's population of nearly eight billion people without the supply infrastructure to support it bore down like an anvil on Wile E. Coyote.

Australia closed its borders, blacked out the internet and prepared to hunker down, down under. What little news that did trickle out was about the same as everywhere else. Densely packed Asia already hard pressed to feed itself, fell into chaos and famine quickly. Europe, who relied heavily on food imports, quickly depleted their food supplies. South American Socialist Governments that were already plagued by shortages were quickly ousted by powerful cartels who in turn found out that you couldn't eat cocaine, heroin or marijuana. Africa suffered a similar fate, exacerbated by religious zealotry and inter-tribal rivalry. Only the Polar Regions suffered little. Mostly because there were so few people to suffer, but since there was no way to supply even those few, they succumbed rapidly.

The United States and Canada fell almost as quickly. Already affected by the food shortages and anarchy, the lifeblood of America drained away when all financial markets collapsed. The great depression of the 1930s was a mosquito bite compared to this debacle. The rich and powerful - "The One Percent Club," as they had been dubbed, found out fast that money with no value wielded no power. Riots broke out in every major city and the medium and small ones too. Already crowded by increased urbanization, the eventual result was predictable. Masses of people, many of them armed, fighting to survive for a few more wretched days or weeks. Looters weren't toting away TV's and jewelry; they were toting assault rifles looking for a local Walmart Super Center food department to take over. Without the trains and trucks to restock the shelves, this became a short-term solution.

***

Hyo had just read these internet headlines to Ki when they met their violent end. Fish and shellfish catches stopped when the big animals rebelled. Schools of fish avoided boats and trawlers. Lobsters and crabs simply refused the bait and moved off. He and his wife and sister-in-law had survived on kelp, seaweed and fish that didn't seem to mind being caught in the small coastal village to which they had fled. Like the other designees, they were ignored by the larger and more dangerous animals. Unfortunately a few passing and famished neighbors noticed, and Hyo's old Korean Army service rifle didn't have enough ammunition.

- MARTIAL LAW DECLARED WORLDWIDE.
  The U.N. disbanded.
- ARMIES DISINTEGRATE FOR LACK OF SUPPLIES
  Weapons used to seize food.
- EPIDEMIC DISEASES OLD AND NEW SPREAD
  Typhus, cholera, Ebola, West Nile virus, and malaria
  spread. W.H.O. disperses
- ATLANTA CENTER FOR DISEASE CONTROL
  Filled only with the dead. - Cause unknown.
- SEED CROPS AND BREEDING STOCK CONSUMED
  BY A STARVING HOARDS
- CROPS ROT IN THE FIELDS
  No way to transport them.
- WIDESPREAD CANNIBALISM REPORTED
  India, Pakistan and China worst hit but also reported
  world wide
- HUMAN CORPSES CONTAMINATE WATER SOURCES
  Infectious disease spreads rapidly
- POWER GRIDS START TO COLLAPSE
  Lack of people to maintain them.

One by one, web sites, news and social media began to disappear. The internet in The United States, that last bastion of truth, justice and the American way was the last to go dark. Some of the more bizarre headlines the "chosen ones" read were:

- ARMED CITIZENS BURN DOWN CAPITOL
  Congress was in session
- CHRISTIAN SECT HAILS SECOND COMING
  while looting St. Mary's food bank.
- CALIFORNIA AND MIDWEST MEGA FARMS PILLAGED
- BILLIONAIRE GROUP promising financial stability based
  on the gold standard die in a hail of lead.

THE CLEAN UP CREW

With the internet gone, news came to the survivors in a more visceral and personal way. Like many, Marco and Antonia noticed that the animals, large and small had offered them no harm although jaguars, boars, bovine and equine critters had killed or chased away almost all others in their vicinity. Even more mysterious than that, even though they lived in a tropical region adjacent to the rain forest, the constant mosquito, chigger, and other ubiquitous insect bites and stings they were accustomed to stopped.

Army ants swarmed in columns, heading toward settlements and cites. They cleaned up carcasses along their way. While gathering edible wild fruits and tubers one day, they were surprised to find a recently deceased human corpse only half eaten by insects and small animals. Their astonishment was because of the observation that where still in evidence, the skin of the dead man revealed countless bee and wasp stings. Hundreds of dead Africanized honeybees littered the ground although they could find no sign of a hive nearby.

Tanner and his brother Michel migrated east out of the Mojave Desert, looking for edibles and a more hospitable climate. They travelled with a small train of wild burros they found in the hills of a California/Arizona border ghost town of Oatman, AZ. Ironically, once a "ghost town tourist attraction" it was now truly a ghost town, save for the burros who were such a hit with the tourists. They had been there when they were eight and ten respectively on a trip with their parents and were curious to ask their dad why the burros had five legs. They had laughed their butts off when he explained.

Burros are ideal pack animals in arid regions, capable of doing without water for long periods and carrying a proportional load that a mule or horse would balk about. Since they were oddly tractable enough, they appropriated six to carry their few belongings and occasionally themselves when feet got sore and tired. They had a short-term destination in mind also.

"I wonder if Dad's cabins are intact," Michael said. "We should at least stop and see since we are heading in that general direction."

"Why not," replied Tanner, "we have time and nowhere else urgent to go. Maybe we will run into some other survivors on the way. The message was sent to many."

The general direction was across the high juniper country of Northern Arizona and it took them seven days to get there. Passing through empty cities like Kingman, they arrived in the tiny hamlet of Ash Fork, only 10 miles from the cabins.

Before they headed up into the hills, they paused and rummaged through town to see if there would be any useful salvage. There was a small amount of canned and dry foods, and a stash of ammo, some of which fit two of the guns they were toting. They also found some less appealing artifacts. Many houses had rat gnawed human skeletons, many of which showed damage prior to the depredation of the rats. Broken arms and shattered skulls, some were grouped together as though huddling to stay warm and not a few in pieces on the floor or still in cook pots by a fireplace.

As they were getting ready to head back, Michael found Tanner standing over and intently studying a skeleton, virtually intact, as it lay reclined in a rotting over-stuffed chair, a dusty bottle of Budweiser on one end table, a pack of cigarettes and a revolver on the other and the skeleton of a small dog in its lap. The scene stayed in Tanners's head for a long time as he pondered what the story behind it was. Had the man died and his faithful companion pined away for him until he died? Had the dog died and the man sat with him until he, himself had died? Was the gun involved or was it, like many others they found, simply left handy just in case? Maybe he, or even she, for Tanner was no forensic expert, shot the dog and then himself. He would never know, nor would anyone else but the skeleton, and it wasn't talking, except in Tanners's dreams for the next few days.

The pair camped out on the high school football field that night and arrived at their father's cabin by mid-morning the following day.

"Good grief, Dad sure had this place locked down," Tanner lamented.

"Not to worry bro, I could always break into our house in Phoenix, so this should be cake," Michael replied with a big grin on his face. Five minutes later, they entered the cabin. Their father Franklin moved permanently to the cabins when his wife passed a few years back. It was small, totally off grid and rustic, resembling a western man-cave. The brothers looked about for some note or clue as to his whereabouts but found nothing but his eclectic collection of memorabilia and his bookshelf.

"Hey, Michael, here's all the books the old man wrote. I read a few of them." Tanner pulled one from the shelf and thumbed through the pages until he found the passage he was looking for. "I remember this part pretty well. Pops and his father predicted some of this crap years ago."

Tanner read aloud as his brother busied himself checking out the food supply cabinet:

"Oddly enough, Barth remembered the numbers. It took until about 1800 - the time of Napoleon for the world population to reach approximately 1 billion. That was from the time that Stone Age man had crawled out his cave until that date. Like, maybe 5,000 some-odd years give or take a millennium. By 1930, it had doubled to 2 billion - 130 years - and doubled again by around 1970 to 4 billion - 40 years. The world continued to add people - about a billion more from 1970 - 1987 - FIVE billion. Projected population (that's projected mind you) by 2025 was 8 billion... 54 years - slightly less than a vertical climb but damn close."

"Well, that won't be a problem now will it?" Michael had been taking stock of the supplies. "I suppose these survived because who the hell other than us would tramp up here? The chow should last us at least a month or two and he stockpiled a lot of ammo and guns too. Let's stay a few days to give the burros a chance to feed and rest and then keep moving east. This is hard living here, and too dry to grow much."

***

Mogambi and Omarra also noted the absence of insect pests, at least as far as they were concerned. They determined to stay put. The compound was now empty except for them and their daughter and the planting season was upon them. The food stocks would last until they got a crop in. Besides, tramping around in Central

Africa with a small child in tow seemed like a bad plan. Game would be plentiful also, although they were loathe to hunt very often because the wild animals, like the insects had left them alone.

"Do you hear that?" Omarra said to her husband late one night. Springing to instant wakefulness, Mogami reached for the shotgun that now was always on his side of the bed. Little Neeta slept between them. The grating noise was faint, but clearly coming from inside the compound.

"Get your revolver and wait for me here," he said as he slipped silently toward their door.

Omarra retrieved her small gun and hastened Neeta under the bed with a whispered admonition for her to stay there. Scant minutes moved along like hours each one putting her further and further on edge. Suddenly, she heard the high crack of a rifle, followed by two shotgun blasts and the night again fell silent. Holding the revolver firmly in two hands, she held it pointed at the door. Floorboards in the adjacent room creaked and as the door swung open, she fired.

"Damn, woman, you almost took my head off!" Mogambi cried, "My own damn fault though for just walking right in. I should have spoken up!"

"Damn right," Omarra replied trembling. "What happened?"

"It was that big ass Swede poacher Karl Malbihn the Park Patrol was looking for. They had posters out about him if you remember. He was stuffing his face with the plantains and melons you had in a bowl on the counter in the kitchen when I came in. Just turned on me with wild eyes and shot at me immediately. I didn't have much choice but to shoot back. The poster described him as six foot three and 265 pounds but by the look of him he was no more than 150 tops. His matted blonde beard was full of stickers and he had bug bites and stings everywhere skin showed. His face was red with boils and fever too. How the hell, he survived in the bush this long is a mystery to me, but he's deader than shit now. Maybe deader.

They took note, like many others, that soon the insects began to sting, bite and crawl on them but no more than normal. Omarra looked at the calendar that hung in their small kitchen and said, "Forty days on the nose since we got the strange messages and the world began to turn upside down."

Mogambi replied, "Or maybe set right side up?"

COLLATERAL DAMAGE

Some of the survivors designated by the babbling being in the orb did indeed opt out or opted out involuntarily. The stage was set and the wheels set in motion, but micro management was not in the cards.

***

Serge and Olga in the deep woods of the Ukraine were the first. Olga awoke one morning to severe abdominal pains that made her normal menstrual cramps seem like nothing more than mild indigestion. Three days later, her appendix ruptured and she died in agony in Serge's arms. Overcome by grief and loneliness, Serge opted out with his Makarov 9mm pistol two days later.

***

Colin Campbell and his wife holed up in their ancestral estate in Northern Scotland. Unfortunately, the strict gun control measures he voted for in the United Kingdom left him unprepared to hold the castle from swarms of starving Britons. With no Bobbies to protect them, they became dinner and a light breakfast the following morning.

***

Hudson Zsu, an archeologist working on a fossilized nest of Ankylosaurus eggs on the fringe of the Gobi Desert actually saw the orb land. He got so busy taking notes and pondering the phenomenon he failed to prepare himself and died of thirst in the heat and cold of the Gobi. His bones eventually got as dry and brittle as the dinosaur eggs he was studying.

***

A dozen more were prey to normal minor mishaps that with no doctors and hospitals were fatal. A military man would call this collateral damage. They didn't exactly see it that way.

DEUX EX MACHINA

At least in the northern hemisphere, the six-month estimate, by the creature in the orb was wrong. Perhaps it was taking an overview, because it was still winter in the far southern climes. Trillions of insects and arachnids wreaked terrible vengeance on their human nemesis and oppressors. Stings, bites and intentional spreading of infectious diseases finished what famine began. A few wretched survivors like the unfortunate Karl Malbihn managed to eek out life, extending a miserable existence for a short time before succumbing to hunger, disease or a sudden fatal encounter with a venomous critter. Alternatively, in some cases, an encounter with a shotgun.

******

"That worked out well don't you think?"

"Mostly and faster than you thought."

"I wonder if they will understand?"

"Maybe a few reminders or guidelines are in order?"

"They will certainly have to be more obvious this time, don't you think?"

"Probably, even though these creatures are more advanced in some ways than their distant progenitors, they are capable of self delusion and aggrandizement. Free will and ego are poor partners."

"I-Gos, I do think you are right. Subtlety is not the route to pursue. When I return, I don't want to see a repetition of the mess I found."

This line of mono-sided conversation continued as the orb silently lifted itself out of the sands of the Mongolian desert. No need for stealth or concealment was needed or desired. The plan decided upon, the alien orb moved slowly at low altitude visible to all below as it passed. A traveler perhaps in some future time would find only a crater about the size of the meteor crater in Arizona. Theories and conjecture would run rampant but none would come close to the truth.

*****

Caitlyn woke up on a sunny Iowa morning in early May. Her sleep was deep and untroubled unlike so many other nights, but she saw a note on her nightstand that was clearly in her own handwriting. Meghan was already awake and coffee was brewing on the woodstove in the kitchen, a small piece of paper lying next to her cup. Her boots were muddy from an early morning foray into the back forty, harrowing with an old mule powered machine, for the new crop of corn.

"This is real odd," Caitlyn began, until she glanced at the paper on the table.

"You think?" Meghan interrupted as they compared the two. Both were identical save for the handwriting and they read:

1. *There is a God, his evidence is everywhere,*
    but you know nothing of him except you are not him.
2. *Acceptance of all good and bad is the key to happiness.*
    Seek not fame, blame or revenge.
3. *Forgiveness is important for you, not your transgressor.*
4. *Make quick amends for times you transgress on others.*
5. *Accumulate only what is needed, no more.*
6. *Waste nothing. Use resources sparingly.*
7. *Sail your own ship, not someone else's*
8. *Do not over breed lest you become a burden to*
    yourselves and your world as you did in the past.
9. *Treat all others, as you would want to be treated yourself*
10. *Send forward all goodness you receive*
    times three to others.
11. *Your lives are finite. Use yours wisely.*
12. *Practice all these principles and share them with others.*
    Follow these simple guidelines and you will need
    no other rules.

"I wonder if this has to do with the unusual full moon we saw on the horizon around dusk last night?" Meghan said.

"Does it matter at this point?" her friend replied. "With all the crazy shit that's happened in the last several months I'm beyond questioning or caring. It is what it is."

"Don't start getting all existential on me Caitlyn, because it's your turn to milk the cows."

Three days later, Caitlyn was working up a good sweat, pumping water by hand from their small well when startled by a voice behind her.

"You know, there is a perfectly good deep well and stock tank next to your gate that only needs some power. There are some solar panels on top of a roof in a town that we just passed by. With a little help, I can rig up a pump that will save you a lot of work. Did it once before when I was working on a ranch in New Mexico."

"Hey bro, my map says we're in heaven," said Tanner who was standing directly behind Michael. "In case you don't remember, according to that old movie Pops made me watch, that means Iowa."

Caitlyn turned to see the brothers but also noticed Meghan standing on their porch with a shotgun, so she regarded the two without fear. Other than a trio of half starved marauders that she drove off with her rifle, they were the first people she had seen in months.

"We could use some help, *and* some company," she added when she saw the clean and open good looks of the two young men. "But we've got some serious rules here."

"Lemme guess," replied Michael, as he pulled a small piece of paper from his hip pocket and handed it to her. Something like these?" His mouth didn't smile but his eyes did. "My brother and I travelled here looking for some rich farmland all the way from the deserts of California and Arizona. Every major building or stone edifice in every deserted town or city we passed had this etched on it. I guess it's something we're supposed to remember, don't you think?"

Caitlyn for once, was at a total loss for words, but Michael launched into a long litany of things he could do to help improve the production and ecological efficiency of their farm in terms that she could barely pronounce, much less understand.

As she stood listening, Meghan lowered her gun and approached. Tanner, let his brother hold forth as he shyly looked over at Meghan. He overcame his less than gregarious personality just enough to manage a smile, because he always had a weakness for redheads.

Meghan returned the smile as she set down the shotgun.

ABOUT THE AUTHOR

John Green is originally from Guilderland, NY, but moved to Arizona in 1999 and is a retired graphic designer, advertising art director, copywriter and illustrator. He spends half his time now at his 40 acre off the grid ranch in northern Arizona, occasionally joined by his lovely and forbearing wife Wendy. Many of his stories written there during the quiet starry nights amid the howls of coyotes, hooting owls and things that go bump in the night.

For more information, and other books by this author including his other books, please go to:

www.jgreenbooks.com

OTHER BOOKS BY J. FRANKLIN GREEN

Young Readers:

• THE WIND IN THE JUNIPERS
• LOLA, SAM AND THE JACKALOPE

Apocalyptic Fiction:
• 2035 THE ELEPHANT IN THE ROOM
• STOWAWAY SUZI AND THE HOUSE OF CARDS

Science Fiction:
• ALIEN HEREDITY
• AND THE MEEK SHALL INHERIT

Historic Fiction:
• THE IMMORTAL SERGEANT BACHMAN

Recovery:
• BOOZE & BETRAYAL

Non-Fiction:
• CONFESSIONS OF A GRAPHIC DESIGNER
• EVERYTHING I NEEDED TO KNOW ABOUT LIFE,
I LEARNED ON A BASEBALL FIELD (*Well, Almost*)
• A BABY BOOMERS HISTORY OF GUILDERLAND, NY
  PARTS I, II & III
• THE COMPLETE TOMMY POLITO'S TAVERN

Supernatural mystery:
• ROADSIDE 66
• THE HOUSE IN THE CLOSET

www.ingramcontent.com/pod-product-compliance
Lightning Source LLC
Chambersburg PA
CBHW031329290526
45784CB00014B/2452